CRM MASTERY

BUILDING AND MANAGING STRONG CUSTOMER RELATIONSHIPS

DR. JAGADEESH PILLAI

Made with ♥ on the Notion Press Platform
www.notionpress.com

|| Dedicated to all wisdom seekers around the world ||

ღღღ

Contents

Contents

Prayer

"Om Bhadram Karnebhih Shrunuyaama DevaahBhadram Pashyemaakshabhiryajatraah SthirairangaistushtuvaamsastanoobhihVyashema Devahitam YadaayuhSwasti Na Indro VridhashravaahSwasti Nah Pooshaa VishwavedaahSwasti Nastaarkshyo ArishtanemihSwasti No Brihaspatir DadhaatuOm Shantih, Shantih, Shantih"

The literal meaning of this mantra is: OM. O Gods! Let us hear auspicious words from our ears. O reverent Gods! Let us behold propitious visions from our eyes, let our organs and body be stable, healthy, and strong. Let us do that which is pleasing to the gods in the life span allotted to us. May Indra, inscribed in the scriptures, bring us fortune! May Pushan, the knower of the world, grant us prosperity! May Trakshya, who vanquishes enemies, bestow us with blessings! May Brihaspati bring us success!
OM Peace, Peace, Peace.

About The Author

Dr. Jagadeesh Pillai is a renowned Guinness World Record holder, writer, and researcher hailing from Varanasi, also known as the abode of Lord Shiva. With a Ph.D. in Vedic Science and a range of creative ideas and achievements, he is a true polymath. He is the author of more than 100 books including Research Publications. Although his roots can be traced back to Kerala, the people of Varanasi hold him in high regard and affectionately consider him one of their own.

In 1998, Dr. Pillai was offered a job at Banaras Hindu University, but he left the position after only two months to pursue greater goals in life. He believed that in order to study Indian scriptures and engage in other creative endeavours, he needed to retire from the daily grind of working solely for money at a young age.

He started an export business from scratch, using the knowledge he had gained from a previous job in the industry. His intelligence and unique approach to business led to great success in a short period of time, earning him more in just a decade and a half than he would have in a lifetime working in a government job. Upon the passing of Dr. APJ Abdul Kalam, Dr. Pillai decided to leave the business and dedicate himself to reading, studying, researching, and experimenting.

During his tenure in the export business, Dr. Pillai traveled to over 16 countries, gaining valuable insight and experiencing the world and life in detail.

Dr. Pillai has achieved four Guinness World Records in the following subjects:

"Script to Screen" - In this record, Dr. Pillai produced and directed an animation film within the shortest time possible, breaking the previous record set by Canadians. He has also received numerous national and international awards and recognitions for this achievement.

Longest Line of Postcards - For this record, Dr. Pillai created a line of 16,300 postcards on the occasion of the 163rd anniversary of Indian Postal Day. The event also included a questionnaire about the Indian flag.

Largest Poster Awareness Campaign - Dr. Pillai designed an awareness campaign on the subject of "Beti Bachao - Beti Padhao" (Save the Girl Child - Educate the Girl Child) to achieve this record.

Largest Envelope - In tribute to the Indian Prime Minister's "Make in India" initiative, Dr. Pillai created a 4000 square meter envelope using waste paper to achieve this record.

Attempted - **70000 Candles on a 210 kg Cake** - To celebrate the 70th Indian Independence Day, Dr. Pillai attempted to light 70,000 candles on a 210 kg cake, which was recorded in World Records India.

Attempted - **Documentary on Dhamek Stupa of Sarnath in 17 Languages** - Dr. Pillai attempted to create a documentary on the Dhamek Stupa of Sarnath, dubbing it in 17 different languages. The result of this attempt is currently awaiting confirmation from the Guinness World Records.

Dr. Pillai is skilled in teaching the Bhagavad Gita, a Hindu scripture, and is popular among young people. He has helped many young people improve their lives through his motivational teachings.

In addition to teaching, he has composed and sung numerous Sanskrit Bhajans and patriotic songs.

He has also written and directed several short films and documentaries for awareness campaigns, and has volunteered with the police in both UP and Kerala to spread awareness about various issues through videos and photography.

Incredibly, he has produced and directed over 100 documentaries about the city of Varanasi, all on his own.

He has also helped and guided more than 25 boys and girls to achieve world records through creative and innovative methods. He is a multifaceted person who uses his intellect and the blessings given to him by God to excel in various areas. He is both a teacher and a student, always learning and teaching, and is able to master any subject he comes across.

He is a selfless social activist and motivational speaker who has overcome struggles and failures to become a successful and enthusiastic individual with a rich life experience.

In addition to his work with the Bhagavad Gita, he is also an efficient Tarot card reader, Astro-Vastu consultant, and a talented singer and composer. He has sung the entire Ram Charita Manas and Bhagavad Gita in his own compositions, and has sung the phrase "Lokah Samastha Sukhino Bhavantu" in 50 different languages. He is currently working on a detailed and scientific study of Vedas, Upanishads, Puranas, and the Bhagavad Gita. He has also composed and sung the Hanuman Chalisa and Gayatri Mantra in 108 and 1008 different compositions, respectively.

Awards - Four Times Guinness World Records, Winner of Mahatma Gandhi Vishwa Shanti Puraskar, Mahatma Gandhi Global Peace Ambassador, Kashi Ratna Award, Dr. APJ Abdul Kalam Motivational Person of the Year 2017, Mother Teresa Award, Indira Gandhi Priyadarshini Award, Bharat Vikas Ratna Award, Udyog Ratna Award, Vigyan Prasar Award, Poorvanchal Ratn Samman.

Preface

In today's fast-paced and highly competitive business environment, building and managing strong customer relationships is more important than ever. The ability to understand and meet the needs of customers, and to build long-term relationships with them, is a key driver of business success.

In this book, we explore the various aspects of customer relationship management (CRM) and how it can be used to build and maintain strong customer relationships. We delve into the strategies, techniques, and technologies that are essential for mastering CRM.

This book is designed for MBA students and business professionals who are looking to improve their understanding of CRM and its applications. It provides a comprehensive overview of the field, covering everything from the basics of customer needs and behaviors to advanced topics such as marketing and sales automation, social CRM, and CRM metrics and ROI.

We also explore the unique challenges that small businesses and startups, public sector and non-profit organizations face when implementing CRM and show how CRM can be tailored to their specific needs.

We hope that this book will serve as a valuable resource for those who are looking to improve their customer relationships and drive business success. Whether you are a student, a business professional, or an entrepreneur, the insights and strategies presented in this book will help you to master CRM and build strong, long-lasting customer relationships.

ONE

Introduction to Customer Relationship Management

Introduction to Customer Relationship Management (CRM) is the foundation of any business that wants to establish and maintain long-term, profitable relationships with its customers. CRM is a business strategy that focuses on identifying, attracting, and retaining customers by understanding their needs and preferences. This is accomplished by collecting, analyzing, and managing customer data to improve communication and interactions.

CRM is becoming increasingly important in today's business environment as customers have more options and are more demanding than ever before. Companies need to be able to differentiate themselves and provide a superior customer experience in order to remain competitive. CRM allows businesses to do this by providing a holistic view of the customer and their interactions with the company.

A CRM system is made up of several components that work together to manage customer relationships. These include customer data management, marketing automation, and sales and service management. Customer data management is the process of collecting, storing, and analyzing customer data to gain insights and improve communication. Marketing automation is the use of technology to automate and streamline marketing tasks, such as email campaigns and social media management. Sales and service management is the process of managing the sales and service process, including lead generation, sales forecasting, and customer service.

The benefits of CRM are numerous and include improved customer engagement, increased revenue, and cost savings. By having a better understanding of customer needs and preferences, companies can tailor their marketing and sales efforts to better target their audience. This leads to increased customer engagement and ultimately, increased revenue. Additionally, by automating repetitive tasks and streamlining processes, companies can save time and money.

There are three main types of CRM: operational CRM, analytical CRM, and collaborative CRM. Operational CRM focuses on automating and streamlining business processes, such as sales, marketing, and customer service. Analytical CRM focuses on analyzing customer data to gain insights and improve decision-making. Collaborative CRM involves sharing customer information across different departments and teams to improve communication and coordination.

When implementing a CRM system, it is important to identify business goals and select the right CRM solution. This includes evaluating different CRM software options and selecting one that best fits the needs of the business. Additionally, it is important to ensure proper training and support for employees to ensure the system is being used to its full potential.

CRM is a business strategy that focuses on identifying, attracting, and retaining customers by understanding their needs and preferences. CRM systems are made up of several components that work together to manage customer relationships, and its benefits include improved customer engagement, increased revenue and cost savings. Implementing a CRM system requires identifying business goals and selecting the right CRM solution and providing proper training and support for employees.

"The biggest risk is not taking any risk. In a world that's changing quickly, the only strategy that is guaranteed to fail is not taking risks."

- Mark Zuckerberg

TWO

UNDERSTANDING CUSTOMER NEEDS AND BEHAVIORS

Understanding customer needs and behaviors is a crucial aspect of effective customer relationship management (CRM). By understanding the needs and preferences of customers, businesses can tailor their products and services to better meet those needs and improve the overall customer experience. This can lead to increased customer satisfaction, loyalty, and ultimately, revenue.

There are several ways to understand customer needs and behaviors. One way is through customer research and surveys. These can be conducted through online or offline methods and can provide valuable insights into customer preferences and pain points. Another way to understand customer needs and behaviors is through data analysis. By analyzing customer data, such as purchase history and website behavior, businesses can gain insights into customer preferences and patterns.

It's also important to understand how customer needs and behaviors may change over time. Keeping track of customer interactions and feedback, and monitoring industry trends and customer demographics can help businesses adapt to changing customer needs.

Another way to understand customer behavior is through segmentation, which is the process of dividing customers into groups based on shared characteristics. This allows businesses to better understand the needs and preferences of different customer segments and tailor their marketing and sales efforts accordingly.

Additionally, businesses can use customer relationship management (CRM) software to track and manage customer interactions and data, providing a more comprehensive view of customer needs and behaviors. This can also help businesses automate and streamline customer-related tasks and processes.

Understanding customer needs and behaviors is a critical aspect of effective customer relationship management. By conducting research, analyzing data, and keeping track of customer interactions, businesses can gain valuable insights into customer preferences and adapt to changing customer needs. Segmentation and CRM software can also aid in this understanding and help businesses tailor their products and services to better meet customer needs.

"The best way to predict the future is to create it."

- Abraham Lincoln

ᑭᑭᑭ

THREE

Data Management and Analysis

Data management and analysis are key components of customer relationship management (CRM) that allow businesses to collect, store, and analyze customer data to gain insights and improve communication. By analyzing customer data, businesses can gain a better understanding of customer needs, preferences, and behaviors, allowing them to tailor their products and services to better meet those needs.

Data management involves collecting, storing, and organizing customer data in a central location. This can include demographic information, purchase history, website behavior, and customer interactions. CRM software is often used to manage and store customer data, providing businesses with a centralized view of customer information.

Once the data is collected and stored, it can be analyzed to gain insights. This can be done through various techniques such as segmentation, which divides customers into groups based on shared characteristics, and data mining, which uses statistical techniques to uncover patterns and relationships in the data.

One of the most powerful aspects of data analysis is its ability to predict future customer behavior. By analyzing customer data, businesses can identify trends and patterns that can be used to predict future customer behavior. This allows businesses to proactively address customer needs and improve the overall customer experience.

Additionally, businesses can use the data to personalize their communication with customers. By understanding customer preferences, businesses can tailor their marketing and sales efforts to better target their audience. This can lead to increased customer engagement and ultimately, increased revenue.

Data management and analysis are key components of CRM that allow businesses to collect, store, and analyze customer data to gain insights and improve communication. By analyzing customer data, businesses can gain a better understanding of customer needs and behaviors, allowing them to tailor their products and services to better meet those needs. Additionally, data analysis can be used to predict future customer behavior, personalize communication and increase revenue.

"Your most unhappy customers are your greatest source of learning."

- Bill Gates

ᵖᵖᵖ

FOUR

Customer Segmentation and Targeting

Customer segmentation is the process of dividing customers into groups based on shared characteristics. This allows businesses to better understand the needs and preferences of different customer segments and tailor their marketing and sales efforts accordingly.

There are several ways to segment customers. One way is through demographic segmentation, which divides customers into groups based on characteristics such as age, gender, income, and education level. Another way is through geographic segmentation, which divides customers based on location, such as country, region, or city. Behavioral segmentation, which segments customers based on their behavior, such as purchase history and website interactions, is also possible.

Once customers have been segmented, businesses can use this information to target specific groups with personalized marketing and sales efforts. For example, a business may target older customers with a different product line or message than it would target younger customers.

Customer targeting can be done through various channels such as email, social media, or targeted ads. By understanding customer preferences and behavior, businesses can tailor their message and offer to better resonate with the target segment.

Additionally, customer segmentation can aid in developing customer personas, which are fictional representations of a business's ideal customer. These personas can help businesses understand their customers on a deeper level, and guide their product development, marketing, and sales efforts.

Customer segmentation is a crucial aspect of customer relationship management that allows businesses to better understand the needs and preferences of different customer segments. By dividing customers into groups based on shared characteristics, businesses can tailor their marketing and sales efforts accordingly and increase the effectiveness of their efforts. Additionally, customer segmentation can aid in the development of customer personas which can be helpful in guiding the efforts of the business.

"Innovation distinguishes between a leader and a follower."

- Steve Jobs

FIVE

PERSONALIZATION AND CUSTOMIZATION

Personalization and customization are important aspects of customer relationship management (CRM) that allow businesses to tailor their products and services to meet the specific needs and preferences of individual customers. This can lead to increased customer satisfaction, loyalty, and ultimately, revenue.

Personalization is the process of making products or services unique to a specific individual. This can be achieved through various means such as personalizing the customer experience, customizing products or services, and providing personalized communication. For example, a business may personalize the customer experience by remembering a customer's name, purchase history or browsing history. Personalization can be done through the use of CRM software, which can track and store customer data, allowing businesses to personalize their interactions with customers.

Customization is the process of creating products or services to meet the specific needs and preferences of individual customers. This can include customizing product features, packaging, or messaging. For example, a business may offer customers the option to customize their own products, such as creating a personalized shirt or a custom-made piece of jewelry.

Personalization and customization can be used in conjunction with customer segmentation, which divides customers into groups based on shared characteristics. By understanding the needs and preferences of different customer segments, businesses can tailor their products and services to better meet those needs.

Personalization and customization are important aspects of CRM that allow businesses to tailor their products and services to meet the specific needs and preferences of individual customers. This can lead to increased customer satisfaction, loyalty, and ultimately, revenue. Personalization and customization can be done through the use of CRM software, and can be used in conjunction with customer segmentation to increase the effectiveness of efforts.

"The goal of a business is to create a customer who creates customers."

- Shiv Singh

ღღღ

SIX

CRM in Public Sector and Non-Profit Organizations

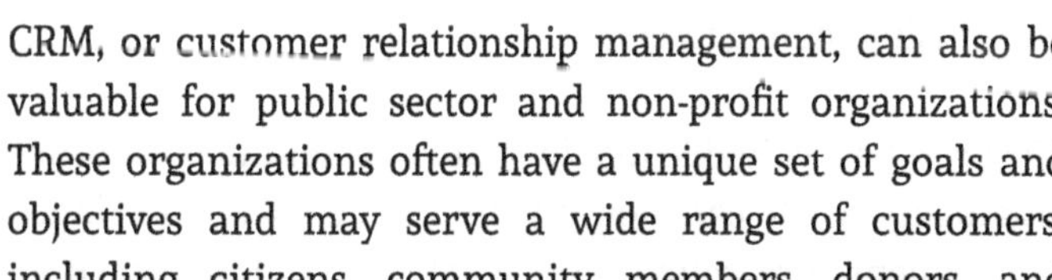

CRM, or customer relationship management, can also be valuable for public sector and non-profit organizations. These organizations often have a unique set of goals and objectives and may serve a wide range of customers, including citizens, community members, donors, and partners. CRM can help these organizations to manage and engage with their various stakeholders more effectively.

In public sector organizations, CRM can be used to manage and improve citizen services. It can help to streamline service delivery and improve the citizen experience by providing a centralized location for managing customer interactions, tracking customer service requests, and providing real-time feedback on service quality.

Additionally, CRM can be used to analyze data and identify patterns to improve service delivery and better understand citizen needs.

Non-profit organizations can also benefit from CRM, particularly in managing donor relationships. CRM can help non-profits to track donations, manage communication with donors, and analyze data to identify patterns and trends in giving. This can help non-profits to improve their fundraising efforts and build stronger relationships with donors. Additionally, CRM can be used to manage volunteer and partner relationships.

In terms of technology, public sector and non-profit organizations have a variety of CRM software options available. Many CRM software providers offer solutions that are tailored specifically for the public sector and non-profit organizations. These solutions often include features such as constituent management, case management, and fundraising management.

CRM can be a valuable tool for public sector and non-profit organizations. It can help to improve citizen and donor engagement, streamline service delivery, and analyze data to better understand the needs of stakeholders. There are many CRM solutions available that are tailored specifically for public sector and non-profit organizations.

"To be successful, you have to have your heart in your business, and your business in your heart."

- Thomas Watson Jr.

SEVEN

Customer Service and Support

Customer service and support are critical components of customer relationship management (CRM) that play a key role in maintaining and building strong customer relationships. These functions involve providing assistance and addressing customer inquiries, complaints, and issues in a timely and effective manner.

Customer service is the process of providing assistance to customers before, during, and after a purchase. This can include answering questions about products or services, providing information about shipping or returns, and addressing customer complaints or issues. Customer service can be provided through various channels such as phone, email, live chat, or social media.

Customer support is the process of providing assistance to

customers after a purchase. This can include troubleshooting technical issues, providing information about product warranties or guarantees, and addressing customer complaints or issues.

Both customer service and support can be improved through the use of CRM software, which can provide a centralized view of customer data, allowing businesses to quickly and effectively respond to customer inquiries and issues. Additionally, by tracking customer interactions, businesses can identify and resolve issues more quickly, and proactively address customer needs.

Having a good customer service and support can increase customer satisfaction and loyalty, leading to increased customer retention and ultimately increased revenue. Additionally, having a good reputation for customer service and support can attract new customers and improve the company's reputation.

Customer service and support are critical components of customer relationship management that play a key role in maintaining and building strong customer relationships. These functions involve providing assistance and addressing customer inquiries, complaints, and issues in a timely and effective manner. By using CRM software, and investing in good customer service and support, businesses can increase customer satisfaction and loyalty, leading to increased customer retention and ultimately increased revenue, as well as attracting new customers and improving the company's reputation.

"Your work is going to fill a large part of your life, and the only way to be truly satisfied is to do what you believe is great work."

- Steve Jobs

ღღღ

EIGHT

CRM Technology and Tools

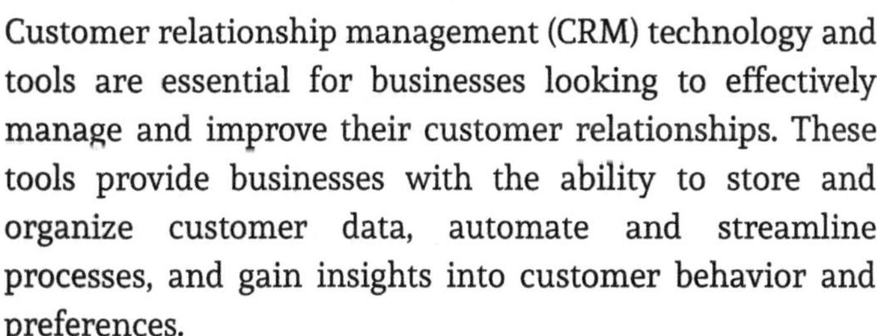

Customer relationship management (CRM) technology and tools are essential for businesses looking to effectively manage and improve their customer relationships. These tools provide businesses with the ability to store and organize customer data, automate and streamline processes, and gain insights into customer behavior and preferences.

CRM software is the most common type of technology used for managing customer relationships. This software typically includes a range of features such as contact management, sales automation, marketing automation, and customer service and support. CRM software can be used to store and organize customer data, automate and streamline processes, and gain insights into customer behavior and preferences.

Other CRM tools include marketing automation software, which can be used to automate and personalize marketing campaigns; analytics and reporting tools, which can be used to gain insights into customer behavior and preferences; and communication and collaboration tools, which can be used to improve communication and collaboration within a business.

Additionally, businesses can also leverage Cloud based CRM systems, which allows business to access their data and system from anywhere, anytime, and with any device. It also allows multiple users to access the system and update the data in real-time.

Implementing CRM technology and tools can help businesses to improve customer satisfaction and loyalty, increase sales and revenue, and gain a competitive advantage. By using CRM software, businesses can improve their ability to store and organize customer data, automate and streamline processes, and gain insights into customer behavior and preferences. Additionally, other CRM tools can help businesses to automate and personalize marketing campaigns, gain insights into customer behavior, and improve communication and collaboration within a business.

CRM technology and tools are essential for businesses looking to effectively manage and improve their customer relationships. These tools provide businesses with the ability to store and organize customer data, automate and streamline processes, and gain insights into customer behavior and preferences. Implementing CRM technology and tools can help businesses to improve customer satisfaction and loyalty, increase sales and revenue, and gain a competitive advantage.

"The best time to plant a tree was 20 years ago. The second best time is now."

- Chinese Proverb

♡♡♡

NINE

MARKETING AUTOMATION

Marketing automation is the use of technology to automate repetitive and time-consuming marketing tasks, such as email campaigns, social media posts, and targeted advertising. This technology helps businesses to streamline their marketing efforts and improve the efficiency of their campaigns.

There are several benefits to using marketing automation. One of the main benefits is the ability to target specific segments of customers. By using customer data and analytics, businesses can create targeted campaigns that are more likely to resonate with specific groups of customers. This can lead to increased conversion rates and higher ROI on marketing campaigns.

Another benefit of marketing automation is the ability to automate repetitive tasks, such as email campaigns and social media posts. This allows businesses to save time and resources, and focus on more strategic tasks.

Marketing automation also allows businesses to personalize their marketing efforts. With the use of customer data, businesses can create personalized messages and offers that are more likely to resonate with individual customers. This can lead to increased customer satisfaction and loyalty.

Marketing automation can be integrated with customer relationship management (CRM) software, which allows businesses to better track and manage customer data. This can help businesses to gain insights into customer behavior and preferences, and create more effective marketing campaigns.

Marketing automation is the use of technology to automate repetitive and time-consuming marketing tasks, such as email campaigns, social media posts, and targeted advertising. This technology helps businesses to streamline their marketing efforts and improve the efficiency of their campaigns. By using marketing automation, businesses can target specific segments of customers, automate repetitive tasks, personalize their marketing efforts, and gain insights into customer behavior and preferences. Integrating marketing automation with CRM software can further enhance the ability of businesses to manage and improve customer relationships.

"Innovation is the specific instrument of entrepreneurship. The act that endows resources with a new capacity to create wealth."

- Peter Drucker

ÞÞÞ

TEN

SALES AUTOMATION

Sales automation refers to the use of technology to automate repetitive and time-consuming sales tasks, such as lead generation, prospecting, and follow-up. This technology helps businesses to streamline their sales efforts and improve the efficiency of their sales process.

One of the main benefits of sales automation is the ability to generate and track leads. By using marketing automation and other tools, businesses can identify and track potential customers, and then use this information to create targeted sales campaigns.

Another benefit of sales automation is the ability to automate repetitive tasks, such as email campaigns and follow-up calls. This allows sales teams to save time and resources, and focus on more strategic tasks such as closing deals.

Sales automation also allows businesses to personalize

their sales efforts. By using customer data and analytics, sales teams can create personalized sales pitches and offers that are more likely to resonate with individual customers. This can lead to increased conversion rates and higher ROI on sales efforts.

Additionally, sales automation can be integrated with customer relationship management (CRM) software, which allows businesses to better track and manage customer data. This can help businesses to gain insights into customer behavior and preferences, and create more effective sales strategies.

Sales automation refers to the use of technology to automate repetitive and time-consuming sales tasks, such as lead generation, prospecting, and follow-up. This technology helps businesses to streamline their sales efforts and improve the efficiency of their sales process. By using sales automation, businesses can generate and track leads, automate repetitive tasks, personalize their sales efforts, and gain insights into customer behavior and preferences. Integrating sales automation with CRM software can further enhance the ability of businesses to manage and improve customer relationships, and increase sales and revenue.

"The best leaders are those most interested in surrounding themselves with what they call 'great people'."

- Jim Rohn

ƤƤƤ

ELEVEN

SERVICE AUTOMATION

Service automation in customer relationship management (CRM) refers to the use of technology to automate repetitive and time-consuming customer service tasks, such as handling customer inquiries, troubleshooting, and resolving issues. This technology helps businesses to improve the efficiency and effectiveness of their customer service efforts.

One of the main benefits of service automation in CRM is the ability to handle customer inquiries and requests quickly and efficiently. By using automated tools such as chatbots, businesses can respond to customer inquiries in real-time, without the need for human intervention. This can improve customer satisfaction and loyalty.

Another benefit of service automation in CRM is the ability to automate repetitive tasks, such as troubleshooting and issue resolution. This allows customer service teams to save time and resources, and focus on more strategic tasks such as building long-term customer relationships.

Service automation in CRM also allows businesses to personalize their customer service efforts. By using customer data and analytics, customer service teams can create personalized responses and solutions that are more likely to resonate with individual customers. This can lead to increased customer satisfaction and loyalty.

Additionally, service automation in CRM can be integrated with other systems, such as marketing automation and sales automation, to create a more seamless and integrated customer experience. This can help businesses to better track and manage customer data, and create more effective customer service strategies.

Service automation in customer relationship management (CRM) refers to the use of technology to automate repetitive and time-consuming customer service tasks, such as handling customer inquiries, troubleshooting, and resolving issues. This technology helps businesses to improve the efficiency and effectiveness of their customer service efforts. By using service automation in CRM, businesses can handle customer inquiries and requests quickly and efficiently, automate repetitive tasks, personalize their customer service efforts, and integrate customer service with other systems. This can help businesses to build long-term customer relationships, increase customer satisfaction and loyalty, and improve overall customer experience.

To be a good leader, you must be able to understand and relate to the people you are leading."

ᑭᑭᑭ

TWELVE

SOCIAL CRM

Social CRM (customer relationship management) refers to the use of social media and other digital channels to manage and improve customer relationships. This approach allows businesses to engage with customers in real-time, and gain insights into their needs and preferences.

One of the main benefits of social CRM is the ability to engage with customers in real-time. By using social media platforms, businesses can respond to customer inquiries and complaints in real-time, and address issues before they escalate. This can improve customer satisfaction and loyalty.

Another benefit of social CRM is the ability to gain insights into customer needs and preferences. By monitoring social media conversations and analyzing customer feedback, businesses can gain valuable insights into customer behavior and preferences. This can help businesses to create more effective marketing and sales strategies.

Social CRM also allows businesses to personalize their interactions with customers. By using customer data and analytics, businesses can create personalized messages and offers that are more likely to resonate with individual customers. This can lead to increased conversion rates and higher ROI on marketing efforts.

Additionally, social CRM can be integrated with other systems, such as marketing automation and customer service automation, to create a more seamless and integrated customer experience. This can help businesses to better track and manage customer data, and create more effective customer engagement strategies.

Social CRM (customer relationship management) refers to the use of social media and other digital channels to manage and improve customer relationships. This approach allows businesses to engage with customers in real-time, and gain insights into their needs and preferences. By using Social CRM, businesses can engage with customers in real-time, gain insights into customer needs and preferences, personalize their interactions with customers, and integrate customer engagement with other systems. This can help businesses to build long-term customer relationships, increase customer satisfaction and loyalty, and improve overall customer experience.

"The most important thing in communication is hearing what isn't said."

- Peter Drucker

ᑭᑭᑭ

THIRTEEN

MOBILE CRM

Mobile CRM (customer relationship management) refers to the use of mobile technology to manage and improve customer relationships. This approach allows businesses to engage with customers on-the-go, and gain insights into their needs and preferences.

One of the main benefits of mobile CRM is the ability to engage with customers on-the-go. By using mobile apps and other mobile technology, businesses can respond to customer inquiries and complaints in real-time, and address issues before they escalate. This can improve customer satisfaction and loyalty.

Another benefit of mobile CRM is the ability to gain insights into customer needs and preferences. By using mobile apps and other mobile technology, businesses can gather customer data and feedback, and analyze it to gain valuable insights into customer behavior and preferences. This can help businesses to create more effective marketing and sales strategies.

Mobile CRM also allows businesses to personalize their interactions with customers. By using customer data and analytics, businesses can create personalized messages and offers that are more likely to resonate with individual customers. This can lead to increased conversion rates and higher ROI on marketing efforts.

Additionally, mobile CRM can be integrated with other systems, such as marketing automation and customer service automation, to create a more seamless and integrated customer experience. This can help businesses to better track and manage customer data, and create more effective customer engagement strategies.

Mobile CRM (customer relationship management) refers to the use of mobile technology to manage and improve customer relationships. This approach allows businesses to engage with customers on-the-go, and gain insights into their needs and preferences. By using mobile CRM, businesses can engage with customers on-the-go, gain insights into customer needs and preferences, personalize their interactions with customers, and integrate customer engagement with other systems. This can help businesses to build long-term customer relationships, increase customer satisfaction and loyalty, and improve overall customer experience.

"The best leaders are those most interested in surrounding themselves with what they call 'great people'."

- Jim Rohn

FOURTEEN

E-COMMERCE AND OMNICHANNEL CRM

E-commerce and Omnichannel CRM (customer relationship management) refers to the use of technology and digital channels to manage and improve customer relationships across all touchpoints of a customer's journey. This approach allows businesses to connect and engage with customers through multiple channels, including online, in-store, and mobile.

One of the main benefits of e-commerce and Omnichannel CRM is the ability to connect with customers across all touchpoints. By using e-commerce platforms and other digital channels, businesses can interact with customers on their preferred channel, and provide a consistent experience across all touchpoints. This can improve customer satisfaction and loyalty.

Another benefit of e-commerce and Omnichannel CRM is the ability to gain insights into customer needs and preferences. By using customer data and analytics, businesses can gather customer data from various channels, and analyze it to gain valuable insights into customer behavior and preferences. This can help businesses to create more effective marketing and sales strategies.

E-commerce and Omnichannel CRM also allows businesses to personalize their interactions with customers. By using customer data and analytics, businesses can create personalized messages and offers that are more likely to resonate with individual customers. This can lead to increased conversion rates and higher ROI on marketing efforts.

Additionally, E-commerce and Omnichannel CRM can be integrated with other systems, such as marketing automation and customer service automation, to create a more seamless and integrated customer experience. This can help businesses to better track and manage customer data, and create more effective customer engagement strategies.

E-commerce and Omnichannel CRM (customer relationship management) refers to the use of technology and digital channels to manage and improve customer relationships across all touchpoints of a customer's journey. This approach allows businesses to connect and engage with customers through multiple channels, including online, in-store, and mobile. By using E-commerce and Omnichannel CRM, businesses can connect with customers across all touchpoints, gain insights into customer needs and preferences, personalize their interactions with customers, and integrate customer engagement with other systems. This can help businesses to build long-term customer relationships, increase customer satisfaction and loyalty, and improve overall customer experience.

"The only limit to our realization of tomorrow will be our doubts of today."

- Franklin D. Roosevelt

♡♡♡

FIFTEEN

CRM METRICS AND ROI

CRM metrics and ROI (return on investment) refer to the measurement and evaluation of the effectiveness and efficiency of a company's customer relationship management efforts. These metrics and measurements are used to determine the value and success of a company's CRM strategies, and to identify areas for improvement.

Some of the key CRM metrics that companies use to measure the success of their efforts include:

Customer retention rate: This measures the percentage of customers that continue to do business with a company over a specific period of time. A high retention rate indicates that a company's CRM strategies are effectively keeping customers engaged and satisfied.

Customer lifetime value: This metric calculates the total revenue a company can expect to receive from a customer over the course of their lifetime. A high lifetime value indicates that a company's CRM strategies are effectively building long-term, profitable relationships with customers.

Net Promoter Score (NPS): This metric measures a customer's likelihood to recommend a company's products or services to others. A high NPS indicates that a company's CRM strategies are effectively building customer loyalty and advocacy.

Sales conversion rate: This measures the percentage of leads or potential customers that are converted into paying customers. A high conversion rate indicates that a company's CRM strategies are effectively closing sales and increasing revenue.

In addition to measuring the success of CRM efforts, companies also use ROI calculations to determine the financial value of their CRM strategies. This involves comparing the costs of a CRM system or initiative to the resulting revenue or cost savings.

CRM metrics and ROI (return on investment) refer to the measurement and evaluation of the effectiveness and efficiency of a company's customer relationship management efforts. These metrics and measurements are used to determine the value and success of a company's CRM strategies, and to identify areas for improvement. Commonly used metrics include customer retention rate, customer lifetime value, net promoter score, and sales conversion rate, along with ROI calculations to determine the financial value of CRM strategies.

"Positive anything is better than negative nothing."

- Elbert Hubbard

ꝥꝥꝥ

SIXTEEN

CUSTOMER COMPLAINTS AND FEEDBACK MANAGEMENT

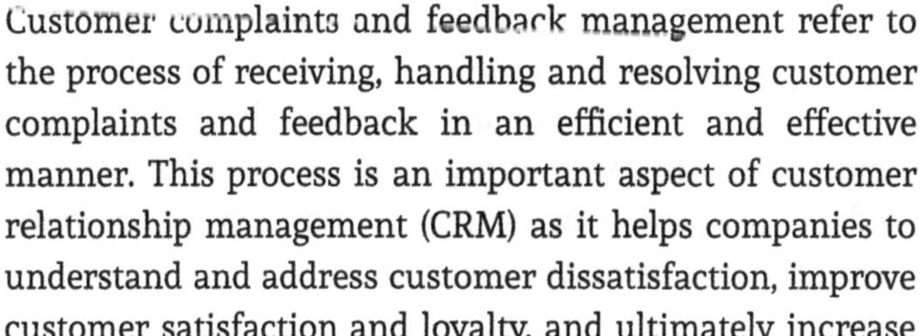

Customer complaints and feedback management refer to the process of receiving, handling and resolving customer complaints and feedback in an efficient and effective manner. This process is an important aspect of customer relationship management (CRM) as it helps companies to understand and address customer dissatisfaction, improve customer satisfaction and loyalty, and ultimately increase revenue.

One of the key steps in customer complaints and feedback management is to establish a clear and efficient process for receiving and handling complaints and feedback. This can include setting up a dedicated customer service or support team, as well as providing multiple channels for customers to submit complaints and feedback, such as phone, email, or social media.

Another important aspect of customer complaints and feedback management is to provide timely and appropriate responses to complaints and feedback. This includes acknowledging receipt of a complaint or feedback, providing an estimated time frame for resolution, and keeping the customer informed throughout the process.

In addition, companies should use customer complaints and feedback to identify and address underlying issues or problems that are causing dissatisfaction. This could include issues with products or services, policies, or processes. By identifying and addressing these issues, companies can improve the overall customer experience and reduce the likelihood of future complaints.

Furthermore, companies should also use customer complaints and feedback as an opportunity for continuous improvement. This includes analyzing customer complaints and feedback data to identify patterns and trends, and using this information to make changes to products, services, policies, or processes that will improve the customer experience.

Finally, companies should also provide a feedback management system that allows customers to provide feedback in a structured and easy way. This can be done by using a survey or a form which can be filled out by the customer.

Customer complaints and feedback management is an

important aspect of customer relationship management (CRM) as it helps companies to understand and address customer dissatisfaction, improve customer satisfaction and loyalty, and ultimately increase revenue. This process involves establishing a clear and efficient process for receiving and handling complaints and feedback, providing timely and appropriate responses, identifying and addressing underlying issues, using customer complaints and feedback as an opportunity for continuous improvement, and also providing a feedback management system that allows customers to provide feedback in a structured and easy way.

important aspect of customer relationship management (CRM) that helps businesses to understand and address customer concerns, improve customer satisfaction and loyalty, and ultimately increase revenue. This process involves establishing a clear and efficient process for receiving and handling complaints and feedback, providing timely and appropriate responses, identifying and addressing underlying issues causing customer complaints and using feedback [illegible] to drive continuous improvement. [illegible] a feedback management system [illegible] to improve [illegible] feedback [illegible] [illegible].

"When one door of happiness closes, another opens, but often we look so long at the closed door that we do not see the one that has been opened for us."

- Helen Keller

♡♡♡

SEVENTEEN

CRM IN B2B AND B2C

CRM, or customer relationship management, is a strategy and set of techniques used by businesses to manage and improve interactions with customers. This can include everything from acquiring new customers to retaining existing ones and improving customer satisfaction. CRM can be used in both B2B (business-to-business) and B2C (business-to-consumer) contexts, although the specifics of how it is implemented may differ depending on the type of business and the customers it serves.

In B2B (business-to-business) contexts, CRM is often used to manage relationships with other businesses or organizations. This can include managing relationships with suppliers, partners, and other third-party organizations. B2B companies often have complex sales cycles and may have a smaller number of customers than B2C companies, so CRM systems may need to be more robust and tailored to support these needs. In B2B, CRM can be used to manage sales, marketing, and customer service activities. It can also be used to track and analyze customer data, to help identify and target key decision-makers and key accounts.

On the other hand, in B2C (business-to-consumer) contexts, CRM is often used to manage relationships with individual consumers. This can include managing relationships with customers who purchase products or services, as well as managing relationships with potential customers who may be interested in purchasing products or services in the future. B2C companies often have a large number of customers, so CRM systems may need to be able to handle a high volume of customer data and interactions. B2C CRM systems often focus on customer acquisition, retention, and loyalty. CRM can be used to manage marketing campaigns, to personalize customer interactions, and to provide customers with targeted offers and promotions.

CRM can be applied to both B2B and B2C contexts, but the specifics of how it is implemented may differ depending on the type of business and the customers it serves. B2B companies may have a smaller number of customers but with more complex sales cycles, so CRM systems will need to be more robust. B2C companies may have a large number of customers and CRM systems will need to be able to handle a high volume of customer data and interactions, and focus on customer acquisition, retention, and loyalty.

"You are never too old to set another goal or to dream a new dream."

♡♡♡

EIGHTEEN

CRM in Small Business and Startups

CRM, or customer relationship management, can be a valuable tool for small businesses and startups. Small businesses and startups often have limited resources and a need to manage customer relationships effectively in order to grow and succeed. CRM can help small businesses and startups to acquire new customers, retain existing ones, and improve customer satisfaction.

In small businesses and startups, CRM can be used to manage sales, marketing, and customer service activities. It can also be used to track and analyze customer data, to help identify and target key customer segments and improve customer engagement. For example, small business owners can use CRM to segment their customer base into different groups, such as new customers, loyal customers, and at-risk customers. They can then create targeted marketing campaigns and offers for each group, which can help to improve customer retention and increase sales.

Additionally, small businesses and startups can use CRM to automate key business processes, such as lead management, follow-up, and customer support. This can help to save time and resources, and also allows owners to focus on growing their business.

In terms of technology, small businesses and startups have many affordable options for CRM software and tools that are easy to use and implement. Many CRM software providers offer cloud-based solutions that can be accessed from any device, which is ideal for small businesses and startups that may have employees working remotely or on the go. Also, there are many free or low-cost CRM tools available that are designed specifically for small businesses and startups.

CRM can be a valuable tool for small businesses and startups. It can help to improve customer engagement, increase sales and revenue, and automate key business processes. There are many affordable CRM solutions available that are tailored to the needs of small businesses and startups.

Other Books Of The Author

1. The Moments When I Met God
2. Kashiyile Theertha Pathangal
3. GURU GYAN VANI
4. Abhiprerak Gita
5. ASSI SE JAIN GHAT TAK
6. Hopelessness of Arjuna
7. The Soul and It's True Nature
8. Sense of Action (Karma)
9. Action through Wisdom
10. Action through Wisdom
11. THEORY AND PRACTICAL OF EVERY ACTION
12. LOGICAL UNDERSTANDING OF THE SUPREME
13. THE IMPERISHABLE SUPREME
14. Yatra Nishadraj se Hanuman Ghat Tak
15. Yatra Karnatak Ghat se Raja Ghat Tak
16. Yatra Pandey Ghat se Prayagraj Ghat Tak
17. Yatra Ranjendra Prasad Ghat se Dattatreya Ghat Tak
18. YaatraSindhiya Ghat se Gwaliar Ghat Tak
19. Yatra Mangala Gauri Ghat se Hanuman Gadhi Ghat Tak
20. Yatra Gaay Ghat Se Nishad Ghat Tak
21. MAA GANGA, GHATEN EVM UTSAV
22. Ganga Arti Dev Deepavali evam Any Utsav
23. Potentials of Digitalized India
24. VEDIC CONSCIOUSNESS
25. A Brief Introduction to Vedic Science
26. Kashi ke Barah Jyotirling
27. IMPACT OF MOTIVATION
28. Let's have a Milky Way Journey
29. Color Therapy in a Nutshell

30. Rigveda in a Nutshell
31. Yajurveda in a Nutshell
32. Samveda in a Nutshell
33. Atharva Veda in a Nutshell
34. Ayushman Bhava - Ayurveda
35. Srimad Bhagavad Gita and Upanishad Connection
36. Srimad Bhagavad Gita - an attempt to summarize each chapter.
37. Facts and Impact of Nakshatra
38. Astro Gems - NAVARATNA
39. Ekadashi - A Concise Overview
40. A Concise View of Hanuman Chalisa
41. Inspirational Gita
42. Nakshatraranyam
43. Summary of 18 Mahapuranas
44. Synopsis of 18 Upa Puranas
45. Rigvediya Upanishads
46. Shukla Yajurvediya Upanishads
47. Krishna Yajurvediya Upanishads
48. Samavediya Upanishads
49. Atharvavediya Upanishads
50. The Seven Great Sages
51. From Rocket Scientist to President Dr. APJ Abdul Kalam
52. The Visionary's Voice - Quotes of Dr. APJ Abdul Kalam
53. The Wisdom of Swami Vivekananda: Insights and Inspiration from a Legendary Spiritual Teacher
54. Ayurvedic Remedies from the Garden
55. Sages and Seers
56. Rising Strong – Motivational Stories of Women
57. Beyond Flames -Mystery stories of Funeral Ghat Manikarnika
58. The Origins of Tulsi: A Look at the Mythological Roots of the Plant"

59. The Holistic Cow: A Look at the Physical, Spiritual, and Cultural Importance of Cows in India
60. Arts of Healing
61. Exploring the Divine
62. Understanding Five Elements
63. The Etymology of Ram
64. Symbols of India
65. Voice of Change (About Speeches of Great Men)
66. She Speaks (About Speeches of Great Women)
67. Patriotism on Celluloid – Brief About Patriotic Films
68. The Music of Motivation: A Brief Guide to Inspirational Film Songs
69. **Unlocking the Secrets of the Dashopanishads**
70. A Cultural Mosaic
71. Ancient Traditions, Modern Minds
72. Ecos of Ancient Wisdom
73. Beneath the Surface
74. From Temples to Ashrams
75. Sages of the Subcontinent
76. The Art of Healling (Ayurveda, Yoga & Naturopathy)
77. Indian Kitchen
78. The Festivals of India
79. The Indian Epics Retold
80. The Power of Mantras
81. The Indian River Ganges
82. The Indian Architecture
83. Rites of Passage
84. The Indian Silk Road
85. The Indian Literature
86. The Indian Villages
87. The Indian Folks & Crafts
88. The Way of Buddha
89. The Ramayan of Tulsidas

90. Astrological Remedies
91. The Secret Power of Motivation
92. Secret of Developing your Inner Strength
93. The Secret Path to Motivation
94. The Art and Secret of Positive Thinking
95. The Secrets of Practicing Ethical Living
96. Indian Art and Painting
97. The Indian Herbalism
98. Bharatanatyam to Kathak
99. Exploring India's Astrological Remedies
100. The Indian Festival of Flowers
101. Indian Handicrafts
102. The Splashes of Joy – India's Colour Festival
103. The Indian Science of Astrology
104. The Indian Mythology
105. Path to Enlightenment
106. The Indian Spirituality for Children
107. Aromas of India
108. The Secrets of Healthy Relationships
109. Ancestral Ties
110. The Indian Street Food
111. Discovering America
112. The Indian Textile
113. Listening to Motivational Speeches
114. Taste of India
115. A Cultural Journey through Indian Nuptials
116. Motivational Quote for Change
117. Secret Strategies for Making Money
118. Secrets to Cultivate a Positive Mindset
119. A Tapestry of Cultures: Exploring India from Kashmir to Kanyakumari
120. Achieving Your Dreams with Resilience: Secret Strategies for Overcoming Obstacles

121. Innovative Startups - 25 Startup Ideas to Spark Your Business Creativity

Contact

DR. JAGADEESH PILLAI

PhD in Vedic Science

Four Times Guinness World Record Holder

Winner of Mahatma Gandhi Vishwa Shanti Puraskar and Global Peace Ambassador

Gemology, Astro & Vastu Consultant - Spiritual Counselor

Consultant for designing World Record Ideas

Efficient Tarot Card Reader

9839093003

myrichindia@gmail.com

drjagadeeshpillai@facebook

drjagadeeshpillai@instagram

jagadeeshpillai@youtube

www. JAGADEESHPILLAI.com

|| LOKAHA SAMASTHAHA SUKHINO BHAVANTU ||

9 798889 5914

Printed by Libri Plureos GmbH in Hamburg, Germany